ideals®
THANKSGIVING

The earth returns its fruitful yields;
The wild geese find the old rice fields;
The turkeys feed; the deer abound;
The dawn is crisp for spotted hound.
Full is the heart and full the living—
Come home, come home; it is Thanksgiving.

—INEZ FRANCK

IDEALS PUBLICATIONS
NASHVILLE, TENNESSEE

A Special Time

June Masters Bacher

It seems so natural somehow,
When colored leaves are due,
To turn thoughts to
     Thanksgiving Day
And people dear to you.

The season is a special time—
A day that's set apart—
For thanking God
     for sending friends
So special to the heart.

Time for Thanksgiving

Virginia Blanck Moore

Have you seen a lot of turkeys
Made of paper, colored brown,
As they strut across the windowpanes
Of schoolrooms round the town?

Have you heard the women talking
At the corner grocery store
Of how the children—scattered wide—
Will all be home once more?

Do you somehow have the feeling,
Now that harvest time is through,
That the Lord in His beneficence
Is mighty good to you?

Then you know it is Thanksgiving time,
That yearly interlude
When we take time and thought to pray
In fervent gratitude.

Row houses in Northwest Portland, Oregon.
Photograph by Steve Terrill

BROWN NOVEMBER

Hal Borland

Those who speak of gray November must be describing their own mood, not the landscape; for this is the season of browns, not grays, the warmest, richest browns of the whole year. The vivid colors of October are past, but they are succeeded by colors that range from the rich golden tan of the sere milkweed leaf to the earth brown of the oak tree's trunk, from the blond ripeness of the corn husk to the lively russet of the apple twig.

Behold the sleek, polished mahogany acorns in their tam-o'-shantered caps of rough country tweed. See the creamed-coffee shells of the hickory nuts. Hold the brown ripeness of a white pine's cone in your hand, and know the bronze spruce needles in the woodland duff. See the key tassels on the box elder, a livelier shade than that deceptive maple's leaves ever achieved. Admire the polished, leathery, maroon-brown pods of the honey locust.

Goldenrod is a brown tangle of stems and tawny plumes at the roadside. Queen Anne's lace has become an intricate ball of weathered copper filigree. Fern fronds are tangles of cinnamon-colored curls, and spore heads of the ostrich fern might have been carved from polished walnut wood. The meadow margin and the fence row are dappled with rust and terra cotta, ginger and snuff, in outworn leaf and crisp stem and ripened seed.

The spectacle of gold and crimson falls and fades, but it leaves no monotone, no colorless gray world. This is brown November, a chromatic triumph as spectacular in its own way as was green April.

The Color of Thanksgiving

Ruth Pitcher

What color is Thanksgiving?
Is it gold and bronze and russet
    autumn leaves?
Or red apples in a barrel?
Is it moist, brown furrows
Of fall-turned fields?
Orange pumpkins
Ripe on the vine?
Purple grapes?
Is it mashed potatoes and cranberries,

Ruby red and creamy white
On a gleaming damask cloth?
And copper flames
That flicker in the blue shadows
    on the hearth?
Or is Thanksgiving
The color of gratitude,
Shades of love
Seen by a thankful heart?

Grapes in Alpine Vineyards, Oregon. Photograph by Dennis Frates

Thoughts on Autumn

Nathaniel Hawthorne

Still later in the season, Nature's tenderness waxes stronger. It is impossible not to be fond of our mother now; for she is so fond of us! At other periods she does not make this impression on me, or only at rare intervals; but in these genial days of autumn, when she has perfected her harvests and accomplished every needful thing that was given her to do, then she overflows with a blessed superfluity of love. She has leisure to caress her children now. It is good to be alive at such times. Thank Heaven for breath—yes, for mere breath—when it is made up of a heavenly breeze like this! It comes with a real kiss upon our cheeks; it would linger fondly around us if it might; but since it must be gone, it embraces us with its whole kindly heart and passes onward to embrace likewise the next thing that it meets. A blessing is flung abroad and scattered far and wide over the earth, to be gathered up by all who choose. I recline upon the still unwithered grass and whisper to myself, "O perfect day! O beautiful world! O beneficent God!" And it is the promise of a blessed eternity; for our Creator would never have made such lovely days and have given us the deep hearts to enjoy them, above and beyond all thought, unless we were meant to be immortal. This sunshine is the golden pledge thereof. It beams through the gates of paradise and shows us glimpses far inward.

Aspen grove near Owl Creek Pass in Uncompahgre National Forest, Colorado. Photograph by Mary Liz Austin/ Austin Donnelly Photography

Thanksgiving

Margaret Sangster

What time the latest flower hath bloomed,
The latest bird hath southward flown;
When silence weaves o'er garnered sheaves
Sweet idyls in our northern zone;
When scattered children rest beside
The hearth, and hold the mother's hand,
Then rolls Thanksgiving's ample tide
Of fervent praise across the land.

And though the autumn stillness broods
Where spring was glad with song and stir,
Though summer's grace leaves little trace
On fields that smiled at sight of her,
Still glows the sunset's altar fire
With crimson flame and heart of gold;
And faith uplifts, with strong desire
And deep content, the hymns of old.

We bless our God for wondrous wealth,
Through all the bright benignant year;
For shower and rain, for ripened grain;
For gift and guerdon, far and near.
We bless the ceaseless Providence
That watched us through the peaceful days,
That led us home, or brought us thence,
And kept us in our various ways.

And if the hand so much that gave
Hath something taken from our store,
If caught from sight, to heaven's pure light,
Some precious ones are here no more,
We still adore the Friend above,
Who, while earth's road grows steep and dim,
Yet comforts us, in tender love,
And holds our darlings close to Him.

Thanks, then, O God! From sea to sea
Let every wind the anthem bear!
And hearts be rife through toil and strife,
With joyful praise and grateful prayer.
Our fathers' God, their children sing
The grace they sought through storm and sun;
Our harvest tribute here we bring,
And end it with, "Thy will be done."

WITH THANKFUL HEARTS
Esther Baldwin York

Let us approach Thanksgiving with a feeling of gratitude for our many blessings—the personal, the universal, the physical, the material, the intangible, the spiritual. They are manifold when we would try to list them. Realizing this, our thanks flow out to our God and to our fellow men. The heart that is thankful is the loving heart, the happy heart, alive and aware!

Hope and Harvest
Margaret Rorke

O God of hope and harvest,
Who gives our daily bread,
Again at this Thanksgiving
We bow a grateful head.
Though corn and grain
   is gathered
In quite a diff'rent way,
We echo with our heartbeats
That first Thanksgiving Day.

We thank Thee, God,
   for planting
That little Pilgrim band
And testing it with hardship
In this untested land;

For sowing with those seedlings
Ideals both strong and just
That caused an infant nation
To breathe, "In God we trust."

We thank Thee, God,
   for giving
The fruits of faith again,
From fields of love and tillage,
From trust in Thee and men.
O God of hope and harvest,
Hear us who humbly pray
And thank Thee for
   Thy blessing
On this Thanksgiving Day.

Gray gambrel barn in New Marlborough, Massachusetts.
Photograph by William H. Johnson

BRAVE AND HIGH-SOULED PILGRIMS,
YOU WHO KNEW NO FEARS,
HOW YOUR WORDS OF THANKFULNESS
GO RINGING DOWN THE YEARS;
MAY WE FOLLOW AFTER;
LIKE YOU, WORK AND PRAY,
AND WITH HEARTS OF THANKFULNESS,
KEEP THANKSGIVING DAY.
—ANNETTE WYNNE

Thanksgiving Day
James J. Montague

With steadfast and unwavering faith, with hard and patient toil,
The Pilgrims wrung their harvest from a strange and sterile soil.
And when the leaves turned red and gold beneath the autumn sun,
They knelt beside the scanty sheaves their laboring hands had won,
And each grave elder, in his turn, with bowed and reverent head,
Gave thanks to bounteous Heaven for the miracle of bread.

And so was born Thanksgiving Day. That little dauntless band—
Beset by deadly perils in a wild and alien land,
With hearts that held no fear of death, with stern, unbending wills,
And faith as firmly founded as the grim New England hills,
Though pitiful the yield that sprang from that unfruitful sod—
Remembered in their harvest time the goodly grace of God.

God grant us grace to look on this, our glorious native land,
As but another princely gift from His almighty hand.
May we prove worthy of His trust and keep its every shore
Protected from the murderous hordes that bear the torch of war;
And be the future bright or dark, God grant we never may
Forget the reverent spirit of that first Thanksgiving Day.

Weathered log barn in Vilas County, Wisconsin.
Photograph by Terry Donnelly/Austin Donnelly Photography

MENUS THROUGH THE YEARS
Diana Karter Appelbaum

The basic traditions of Thanksgiving dinner have not changed since Fannie Farmer offered her 1914 Thanksgiving menu, suggesting roast stuffed turkey, giblet gravy, cranberry molds, curled celery, mashed potatoes, onions in cream, oyster and chicken pie, Thanksgiving plum pudding, hard sauce, mince pie, pumpkin pie, and assorted nuts. Families add a side dish or argue over the relative merits of whole-berry versus jellied cranberry sauce, but only an occasional restless food editor proposes major changes in the menu.

In Miss Farmer's day, food editors suggested such additions as escalloped sweet potatoes with mushrooms, orange and chestnut salad, roast ducks with orange slices and jelly, or pumpkin ice in blossoms. Editors have continued to propose replacing turkey with individual Cornish game hens or omitting potatoes, onions, and peas in favor of asparagus, wild rice, and broccoli. But few cooks pay them heed: broccoli and game hens can grace a festive table any time of the year; sweet potatoes and turkey define Thanksgiving dinner.

It is often pointed out that turkey, cranberries, pumpkin, corn, and potatoes are all native American foods and, for this reason, constitute a fitting repast on our national feast day. There is truth in this reasoning; and it may explain how these foods came to be eaten on Thanksgiving, but it cannot explain why we eat them still.

Thanksgiving Day, the emotions we attach to the holiday, the people we share it with, and the foods we eat on it are hopelessly bound together. Every slice of turkey is a serving of tradition, each ladle of cranberry sauce a pouring out of American history, each slice of pie an offering of love, of family, of tradition, of—Thanksgiving.

Photograph by Jessie Walker

A CONTINUING TRADITION

D. Susan Rutz

*T*he tradition of giving thanks began hundreds of years ago, with two groups of strangers— the Pilgrims and the Native Americans. Since then, we have modified the traditional feast to include football games, naps, and the gathering of families. We look forward to it each year.

Our homes are filled with the wonderful fragrances of pies, breads, and turkey. Our bounty is far more than that first Thanksgiving, but the message has endured. The traditions vary among families, but we all celebrate the same hope— that our family and friends will share in the warmth of God's love and that peace will find its way to our table.

Father, thank You for our bounty, for our table, and for all that lies before us. May we share this time with our family and friends, and may we never forget those less fortunate. Keep those far from home close to our hearts, and bring them safely home again. Amen.

Sugar maple and home in Wayland, Massachusetts.
Photograph by William H. Johnson

PIE-MAKING TIME

Harriet Beecher Stowe

The making of pies . . . assumed vast proportions that verged upon the sublime. Pies were made by forties and fifties and hundreds, and made of everything on the earth and under the earth.

The pie is an English institution, which, planted on American soil, forthwith ran rampant and burst forth into an untold variety of genera and species. Not merely the old traditional mince pie, but a thousand strictly American seedlings from that main stock, evinced the power of American housewives to adapt old institutions to new uses. Pumpkin pies, cranberry pies, huckleberry pies, cherry pies, green-currant pies, peach, pear, and plum pies, custard pies, apple pies, Marlborough-pudding pies—pies with top crusts, and pies without, pies adorned with all sorts of fanciful flutings and architectural strips laid across and around, and otherwise varied, attested the boundless fertility of the feminine mind, when once let loose in a given direction.

Fancy the heat and vigor of the great pan-formation, when Aunt Lois and Aunt Keziah, and my mother and grandmother, all in ecstasies of creative inspiration, ran, bustled, and hurried—mixing, rolling, tasting, consulting—alternately setting us children to work when anything could be made of us, and then chasing us all out of the kitchen when our misinformed childhood ventured to take too many liberties with sacred mysteries. Then out we would all fly at the kitchen door, like sparks from a blacksmith's window. . . .

In the corner of the great kitchen, during all these days, the jolly old oven roared and crackled in great volcanic billows of flame, snapping and gurgling as if the old fellow entered with joyful sympathy into the frolic of the hour; and then, his great heart being once warmed up, he brooded over sucessive generations of pies and cakes, which went in raw and came out cooked, till butteries and dressers and shelves and pantries were literally crowded with a jostling abundance.

A great cold northern chamber—where the sun never shone, and where in winter the snow sifted in at the window cracks, and ice and frost reigned with undisputed sway—was fitted up to be the storehouse of these surplus treasures. There, frozen solid, and thus well preserved in their icy fetters, they formed a great repository for all the winter months; and the pies baked at Thanksgiving often came out fresh and good with the violets of April.

Photograph by Steve Terrill

Family ~ Recipes

LEFTOVERS SANDWICH

1 large (8-ounce) sweet potato, peeled
1 tablespoon water
1 cup bottled turkey gravy
4 sourdough rolls
4 teaspoons dried sage

1 pound thickly sliced roasted turkey,
   torn or cut in 2-inch pieces
1 cup whole- or crushed-berry
   cranberry sauce

Cut sweet potato into ¼-inch slices. Place slices on a plate, sprinkle with 1 tablespoon water, cover loosely with plastic wrap, and microwave on high 6 to 7 minutes or until very soft. In a small saucepan over medium heat, heat gravy about 2 minutes. Split rolls in half and pour 2 tablespoons gravy on each half; sprinkle sage on top. Divide turkey into 4 equal portions and place on the bottom half of rolls. Top with sweet potato slices. Spread cranberry sauce over the top half of rolls and close the sandwiches. Add salt and pepper to taste and serve. Makes 4 servings.

PUMPKIN BREAD

2 cups all-purpose flour
1 teaspoon baking soda
½ teaspoon salt
½ teaspoon nutmeg
½ teaspoon cinnamon
½ teaspoon ginger
1 cup firmly packed light brown sugar

½ cup granulated sugar
1 cup cooked or canned pumpkin
½ cup vegetable oil
2 eggs, beaten
1 cup golden raisins
½ cup chopped walnuts
¼ cup water

Preheat oven to 350°F. In a medium bowl, combine flour, soda, salt, and spices; set aside. In a large bowl, combine brown sugar, granulated sugar, pumpkin, oil, and eggs. Beat until blended. Add flour mixture; blend well. Stir in raisins, nuts, and water. Spoon into greased 9 x 5-inch loaf pan. Bake 65 to 75 minutes or until a wooden pick inserted near the center comes out clean. Cool 10 minutes. Turn out on a wire rack to cool completely.

Apple Pie Streusel

⅔ cup walnuts

½ cup (packed) golden brown sugar

¼ cup yellow cornmeal

¼ cup plus 2 tablespoons all-purpose flour

2¼ teaspoons ground cinnamon, divided

1¼ teaspoons ground nutmeg, divided

5 tablespoons chilled unsalted butter,
   cut into small pieces

2¼ pounds Granny Smith apples (about 6
   medium), peeled, quartered, cored,
   cut into ½-inch-thick wedges

½ cup sour cream

¼ cup granulated sugar

¼ teaspoon ground cloves

1 unbaked 9-inch pie crust

In a processor, combine nuts, brown sugar, cornmeal, ¼ cup flour, ¾ teaspoon cinnamon, and ½ teaspoon nutmeg. Pulse until nuts are finely chopped. Add butter and process until small moist clumps form. (Can be prepared 1 day ahead. Cover and refrigerate.)

Preheat oven to 375°F. In a large bowl, toss apples with sour cream to coat. In a small bowl, mix granulated sugar, 2 table-spoons flour, 1½ teaspoons cinnamon, ¾ tea-spoon nutmeg, and cloves. Sprinkle mixture over apples and toss to coat.

Transfer filling to pie crust. Sprinkle streusel over apples, covering completely. Bake pie until apples are tender and streusel is golden, about 1 hour. Tent pie with foil if streusel browns too quickly. Transfer pie to rack, cool slightly, and serve.

Corn Pudding

2 tablespoons all-purpose flour

1 cup milk, divided

2 large eggs, beaten

1 tablespoon granulated sugar

1 17-ounce can creamed corn

2 tablespoons butter, melted

½ teaspoon vanilla extract

Preheat oven to 350°F. Stir flour into ¼ cup of the milk, making sure no lumps of flour are left. In a medium bowl, combine this paste with remaining milk, eggs, sugar, corn, butter, and vanilla. Pour into a greased 8 x 8-inch pan or 1-quart casserole. Bake until set in the middle, 30 to 40 minutes. The pud-ding will be custard-like when done; a table knife inserted into the pudding should come out clean. Serve hot. Makes 4 to 6 servings.

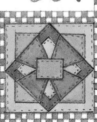

THE KEEPER OF TRADITIONS

Ellen Goodman

*I*t is my turn now: my aunt, the keeper of Thanksgiving, has passed the baton, or should I say the drumstick? She has declared this a permanent legacy. Soon, according to plan, my grandmother's dishes will be delivered by cousin-courier to my dining room. So will the extra chairs and the communal chafing dishes. The tradition will also be transplanted.

But this morning, my aunt has come over to personally deliver a piece of this inheritance. She is making stuffing with me. In one hand, she carries the family Thanksgiving "bible," a small blue book that bears witness to the recipes and shopping lists and seating plans of decades past. In the other hand, she carries three loaves of bread, a bag of onions, and the appropriate spices.

It must be said that my aunt does not quite trust me to do this stuffing the right way, which is, of course, her way and her mother's way. She doesn't quite trust my spices or my Cuisinart or my tendency to cut corners. So, like a tribal elder, she has come to instruct me, hands-on, to oversee my Pilgrim's Progress every step of the way.

Together we chop the onions. Not quite fine enough for her. I chop some more. Together we soak the bread and squeeze it. Not quite dry enough. I squeeze again.

Gradually I, the mother of an adult child, standing in the kitchen of the home I make mortgage payments on, feel myself again a child. Only this time I find amusement in taking instructions from my elder. More than amusement. I find comfort in still being somebody's young.

But sautéing the onions until they are per-fectly brown (my aunt doesn't like white onions in the stuffing), I start divining a subtext to this recipe sharing. It says: *Time is passing. Generations pass. One day I will be the elder.*

"I don't think I like this whole thing," I say aloud, sounding like the child I am now. My aunt, who is about to be threescore years and ten, stops stirring for a moment and looks at me. She understands. And for a while it isn't just the fumes of onions that come into our eyes.

The moment passes; I go back to mixing, and my aunt goes back to her favorite activity: bustling. But I no longer feel quite so much the child.

Adulthood arrives in these small sudden exchanges more than in well-heralded major crises. And the final moment of assuming adulthood may be when we inherit the legacy, become the keeper of traditions, the curator of our family's past and future memories. When the holidays are at our house. The reunions at our instigation. When the traditions are carried on, or cast aside, because of choices we make.

When we were small, my sister and I used to giggle at assorted holiday tables ruled over by our elders. We would at times squirm under the rule of imposed traditions and best behaviors. In time, when we were teenagers and then young parents, we were occasionally rebellious conformists, critical participants at family celebrations. We maintained a slight distance of humorous affection for the habits that the older generation carried on. We were the ones who would point out that no one really liked mincemeat, that the string beans were hopelessly mushy, the onion-ring topping simply passé. It was easy to rebel against the things we could count on others maintaining.

Now I see this from another vantage point, that of almost-elder. I see that tradition is not just handed down but taken up. It's a conscious decision, a legacy that can be accepted or refused. But once refused, it disappears.

How fragile is this sinew of generations. How tenuous the ceremonial ties that hold families together over time and generations. So it is my turn to accept the bequest, the dishes, the bridge chairs, the recipe book. This year there will be no string beans. But the turkey will come with my grandmother's stuffing, my aunt's blessing, and my own novice's promise.

Thankful Hearts
Stella Craft Tremble

We are thankful for the work
    we have,
Regardless of success,
For friends and family
    we love
Who bring us happiness.

For the freedom of religion that
Lessens trouble's scars,
For the hope and vision that
    we have
With eyes upon the stars.

We are thankful for America:
For her mountains and her seas,
For her villages and cities,
For our many liberties.

Now as the old year folds
    its wings,
With gold in every glen,
We thank the Giver of
    all good
For His great love.
Amen!

Thanksgiving
John Manier

Once each year at harvest's end,
Across this land of living,
We rest and feast and spend
One day upon Thanksgiving.

(Our barns and bins can
Hardly hold the fruitful days;
Our God has been good
In every way, as always.)

Wait not until the harvest's end
Of your life with the living;
Each day, each hour,
    a choice to spend
Some new now
    as Thanksgiving.

Bly Farmstand in Wolfeboro, New Hampshire.
Photograph by William H. Johnson

IT'S THANKSGIVING DAY!

Helen Colwell Oakley

No one appreciates the full meaning of Thanksgiving Day more than a farm family. They know firsthand the labor, worry, loving care, and problems that all lead up to a most happy Thanksgiving Day. Mom has been selecting choice tomatoes to keep for a salad on Thanksgiving Day—she makes daily trips to the garden to gather them when they are just right. She has also been setting aside the best squash, smoothest carrots, a beautiful green cabbage, and storing them in the cellar with the crop of winter potatoes and apples. Dad says, "A full cellar is a must on the farm, as there is no telling what the winter will bring!"

The boys have been searching for hickory nuts in the woods so that Mom can make her delicious nut cake for Thanksgiving Day dinner. The girls bring small jars of jellies and jams which they have made for the holidays. By now, the cupboard shelves are filled with pickles, relishes, and dried fruits and nuts. Into the freezer go packages of brown bread and mincemeat cookies. Preparing and storing part of the Thanksgiving menu in advance makes the important day less hectic. Mom has more free time to spend with family and friends. The day before the holiday, Mom makes her famous pumpkin pies with lots of eggs, fresh pumpkin, spices, sugar, and creamy milk from the milk house.

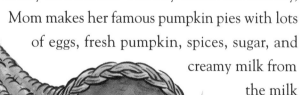

At dawn on Thanksgiving Day, everyone meets at the Blueberry Farm for a light breakfast. Then, when breakfast is cleared away, the turkey is stuffed with old-fashioned stuffing (sage, dried bread crumbs, onion, chopped celery, and a small amount of water). Dad helps to place it in the oven—my, but it is heavy. The country kitchen takes on a festive air; the ovens are all on, and the delicious smells pouring forth say, "It's Thanksgiving Day, once again!" Pumpkin, apple, and mince pies are stacked on the racks, and cranberries are bubbling on the back of the stove. Brown sugar beans are cooking in the crock pot, and Mom is getting ready to pop some baking-powder biscuits into one of the large ovens. A large hubbard squash is almost done and will be scraped out by Dad into a large bowl and mixed with butter—Grandma says that you must have a hubbard squash or you haven't got a Thanksgiving dinner.

Everywhere one looks, it seems to say, "It's Thanksgiving Day!" The little country churches are having special services to offer thanks for our many blessings. The schools have drawings of turkeys, cornstalks, pumpkins, and the horn of plenty overflowing with fruits, vegetables, and nuts. Homes are decorated with dried corn, and stalks are made into a decoration for the front door. Friends and relatives are guests in just about every house in the community—many are spending the entire Thanksgiving holiday, Wednesday through Sunday. Thanksgiving in the country is delightful with family reunions, feasts, hikes in

Red barn and maple in Shelburne, Massachusetts.
Photograph by William H. Johnson

the woodland to get back to nature and, if there is snow, sleigh-riding.

After the feast is over, conversation turns to Thanksgiving Days gone by. Dad recalls, when he was a boy, the faint tinkle of sleigh bells as many guests approached his grandparents' house in the country for a Thanksgiving dinner. A guest recalls the singing tea kettle on her grandmother's black cooking stove and the full wood box nearby. Another guest remembers that she had Thanksgiving dinner at her aunt's house—a large pot of wild game and all the fixings you could hold. There were so many cousins, aunts and uncles, brothers and sisters, and friends that one could barely move. There was usually a feud going on between the relatives—some were not speaking to others. The next reunion on

Thanksgiving Day of the following year would take place with everyone good friends once again—it was something to be thankful for. But after dinner, sparks would fly between the cousins—soon the aunts and uncles would be in on it, and Grandpa would be shaking his fist at everyone; and the feud would be on again. Fortunately, no one held a grudge for long—not with Grandma trying to patch things up. She would relate a sad story about one to the other, and, as they all had soft hearts, they wanted to be friends again. Those were the days—the good times, and, yes, I do miss the feuding too.

Mom says, "We all have so much to be thankful for. This is a happy Thanksgiving Day; may we have many more."

Thanksgiving Night

Wilbur Dick Nesbit

Last night I got to thinking, when I couldn't go to sleep,
Of the way Thanksgiving served me in the days when joy was cheap—
Of how we'd have a turkey, and of how I'd beg a taste
Whenever they would open up the oven door to baste
The bulging breast, and how then from the oven came a drift
Of tantalizing odor, such as only boys have sniffed.

I got to thinking of it—for I couldn't go to sleep—
Of mince pies in the pantry, where I'd sidle in and peep,
And jelly and plum butter, and the peach preserves and cake;
And then I got to thinking of how fine 'twould be to take
A trip back to the old days, when the dancing candlelight
Played pranks with all the shadows on the wall Thanksgiving night.

The boys I used to play with! I could shut my eyes and see
The whole troop of them waiting and a-waving hands to me;
All freckled, ragged trousered, with their scarfs and mittens too,
They made a splendid picture—but the picture wasn't true;
For they've grown up, as I have, and strange paths have lured our feet—
The paths that find tomorrow and that never, never meet.

I wondered if they also were not lying half-awake
And thinking of the turkey and the jelly and the cake;
And if they had their fancies of the lazy little street
That leads beneath the maples where the topmost branches meet.
And suddenly I heard them—heard the murmurs low and clear
That told me they were with me and were very, very near.

Sugar maple and white fence in Bennington, Vermont.
Photograph by William H. Johnson

The Truth about Turkey Soup

Karen Pilibosian Thompson

There was a serious lesson to be learned from a simple bowl of soup.

Today is Thanksgiving and, while the rest of my family enjoys a first, long winter's nap, I am up early to roast the turkey we won in a raffle. This was an exciting event—complete with a trip to the farm offering the prize, a look at the live birds, and our picture in the local newspaper. The farm owners offered us a 40-pounder that they seemed awfully anxious to get rid of (it probably wouldn't have fit in their oven, either). Instead we gratefully accepted the 25-pounder, plenty large enough—and early enough—for me, thank you.

Cooking the Thanksgiving turkey is something the grown-up me has learned to do; it is a welcome rite of passage to be the one to prepare the holiday meal and host the celebration for the family. As I sauté onions and celery (how can it be that an aroma guests find so enticing at dinnertime smells so unappetizing before dawn?), I recall the day I learned the truth about turkey soup. The lesson—which was taught to me by a friend—wasn't painful or hard-won. Like our turkey this year, it was practically free for the taking. And, as the truth often will, it was staring me in the face long before I "got" it.

It was a very ordinary end-of-the-summer midmorning in our small town. My friend had invited me for lunch. Not far from her house was an abandoned granite quarry, and the day was one of those early-autumn days that you sense will be the last really warm one of the year (here in Maine, it usually comes in late September). We decided to go for a swim in the quarry before we ate. The water was clear and painfully icy; after only seconds our heads ached and our arms and legs became numb. We lay on the granite banks in sunshine that was still strong enough to thaw us before we made our way back to the house.

Still shivery inside from the water's chill, I sat at my friend's table, and she served me a bowl of turkey soup. By that time in my life, I had become pretty adept at roasting a turkey, but I had yet to come up with a good turkey soup. For years I had been trying, adding everything I could think of and still not getting it quite right. My friend's turkey soup, though, was perfect. There was no other word for it. Not only did it taste wonderful after our dip in the frigid quarry water, but this was the soup, the one I had been trying for years to discover.

All at once, as I sat at my friend's table, I realized what the trouble was: I had been trying much too hard. This satisfying soup didn't contain every exotic ingredient known to cooks; it was, like my friend, unpretentious and absolutely delightful. It was made with turkey, carrots, and rice—nothing fancy. And it taught me that the truth about turkey soup—and about lots of other things—is that simple is best. The lesson, and the soup, have served me well ever since.

As I work in my quiet kitchen preparing a meal for the hour when my house will be filled with happy mayhem, I am reminded that elaborate things—holidays, food, even lives—are not necessarily the finest ones. I say a small prayer that today, and on all days, I will remember to honor the lesson I found in a simple bowl of turkey soup.

Going Home for Thanksgiving
Angela Gall

A hundred miles of singing road
Where hill-caped farmlands fall and rise
With gaping bins of yellow grain,
Pumpkins gold, and harvest skies;
Then the hill-home the heart knows well,
The warmth where open arms await,
The sweets and spice all nostril-nice,
The turkey-cranberry laden plate—
This feast with loved ones a world away,
All mine by journey of heart today.

IF WE CELEBRATE TOGETHER,
OR MANY MILES APART,
I SHARE THANKSGIVING WITH YOU
IN A CORNER OF MY HEART.
—MONA K. GULDSWOG

Swift River Covered Bridge in Conway, New Hampshire.
Photograph by William H. Johnson

Through My Window

Thanksgiving: Past Imperfect

Pamela Kennedy

We had recently moved away from kith and kin and relocated to a community hundreds of miles from anywhere we'd ever been before. When Thanksgiving came around, we were invited by some new friends to join them and several other upwardly mobile young couples for a holiday dinner—adults only.

It was an evening to remember. The table was set with an exquisite arrangement of spicy gold chrysanthemums and autumn leaves. Bone china and lead crystal gleamed between flatware of shimmering sterling. Crisp linen underlined the settings and crowned each plate. In the serene glow of flickering tapers, we dined on a gourmet menu which included chilled cream of broccoli soup, Cornish game hens in nests of wild rice, artichoke hearts vinaigrette, and—the grand finale—praline bananas en flambé. It was utterly perfect—too perfect. In fact, it was hardly recognizable as Thanksgiving.

For me, Thanksgiving has always been a holiday full of family, confusion, craziness, and characters. The whole day revolves around gratitude and eating—the basics. And when a family gathers together and gets down to basics, strange things happen.

First of all, there are always more people than room. This means innovative seating arrange-

ments must be devised. We always started with a large sheet of plywood on top of the dining room table. This usually created as many problems as it solved. We could seat extra folks, but the table-cloths never quite fit and the table was so wide and long, it was difficult to reach things. Then there was the droop factor. If the plywood was much larger than the table top, it took on a sort of convex appearance where the edges were a bit lower than the center. This was all right until Uncle Fred decided to hunker down with both elbows to get a better purchase on a drumstick. On one such occasion, the creamed onions gave in to gravity and slid gracefully into Grandma's lap.

Children under two were perched on telephone books or in highchairs next to a tolerant relative in washable clothes. From this vantage, the little darlings could pitch everything from salad to creamed peas with alarming accuracy. EFO's (edible flying objects) were always a part of Thanksgiving.

If you were over two but under fourteen, you were obliged to occupy a card table. One leg always threatened to cave in if nudged properly. The best thing about being at a card table, however, was the location, usually in the living room or a spare bedroom and out of earshot of any adults. You could burp, reach across the table, stick pitted olives on all ten fingers, or tell a joke with impunity.

Someone always got the giggles right after taking a drink of milk and more or less saturated things.

Table settings were eclectic. Who had enough dishes and silverware for twenty-five people? The grownups got the good things that matched. The older children got the everyday stuff, but might end up with a salad fork and a tablespoon because the regular size was used up. Little people got divided plastic picnic plates and plastic glasses. The only crystal was in Aunt Edna's brooch. The "good silver" really wasn't. It was plate, in a pattern called "Queen Anne's Lace," and had been purchased with an astronomical number of Betty Crocker coupons.

The Thanksgiving menu was fairly predictable: turkey, candied sweet potatoes, mashed potatoes and gravy, creamed onions, peas and carrots, a fruit salad, dressing, relishes, and pies for dessert. Lots of pies. Everyone brought part of the dinner and it was assembled at the host's home. This usually made for some interesting developments—like the year Aunt Mildred's individual gelatin turkeys melted in the back seat during a traffic jam. I won't relate what the end product looked like, but cousin Ellen's description made for great hilarity and lots of sprayed milk at one of the card tables.

Gratitude was always an integral part of our family gatherings, and everyone was expected to share at least one blessing from the past year. These testimonials were often heartwarming, always interesting, and occasionally questionable. One year Uncle Henry rose solemnly, held up his water goblet, and intoned prayerfully, "I

am extremely grateful that my beloved sister, Ada, has seen fit to spare us from her asparagus crepes this Thanksgiving." He sat down to a chorus of "Amens" and a patient sigh from Ada as she passed this year's offering, zucchini strata.

At our Thanksgiving dinners, the guests were as mismatched as the china. Uncle Richard, a nuclear engineer, chatted amicably with the young gas station attendant who had married one of the cousins. A first-time mother conferred with Great-Grandma about the ageless concerns of colic and cradle-cap. The children, all shapes and sizes, fit into all the niches—empty laps, empty corners, empty arms. It was a holiday that was warm, unstructured, and held together with the adhesive that binds us still—love.

Reflecting now upon it all, I must admit that my new friends' Thanksgiving was delicious and beautiful and wonderfully perfect. But I think if I could choose, I'd opt for my Thanksgivings—past-imperfect. For despite the chaos and confusion, they were always perfectly wonderful.

Thanksgiving Day Is Here

Kay Hoffman

When the turkey's roasting brown
And the pies are cooling near,
When your tastebuds are a-tingling,
Then Thanksgiving Day is here.

Soon the doorbell will be chiming
With a gladsome welcome sound;
All the kinfolk will be coming
From the many miles around.

Who cares if leaves
    have tumbled down
And skies are dark and gray;
The warm, bright smile
    on each dear face
Will brighten up the day.

As heads are bowed
    and thanks are sent
In humble table prayer,
Each one counts
    his daily blessings
Of full and ample share.

Now is the time for catching up
On events both old and new;
What's happening in
    the old hometown?
How are John and Jim and Sue?

Oh, the sound of happy voices
To my heart will ever cling;
When the kinfolk join in song,
How they make the rafters ring!

There's a sprinkling of snowflakes,
And the moon is riding high;
Our goodbyes are
    long and heartfelt,
A tear in many an eye.

A prayer is breathed
    for each loved one
While on the homeward way:
"Take care of these
    dear kinfolk, Lord,
Till next Thanksgiving Day."

Maple tree and stone wall in Homes Country Village, Hillsborough Center,
New Hampshire. Photograph by William H. Johnson

Our Treasured Traditions

CARVING THE TURKEY

Faith Andrews Bedford

Thanksgiving at our house was always a festive affair when I was growing up. While Christmas was reserved for immediate family, Thanksgiving often brought to our table third cousins twice removed, bachelor friends of my father, recently widowed neighbors—anyone we knew who might not have already made plans about where to dine on that special day.

The meal required a full week of preparation. All the leaves had to be added to the dining-room table, and sometimes a card table was placed at the very end. The linens were pressed and the silver polished. Extra chairs were rounded up from any neighbors who could spare a few.

Mother was queen of the kitchen and marshaled my sisters and me like small troops in a grand plan of attack. There was a carefully prepared schedule tacked to the kitchen door. We began cooking three days in advance.

"No one," Mother said, "arranges a relish tray better than Ellen." And so it was that my younger sister welcomed a task that some might have viewed as an onerous chore as an opportunity to display her artistic talent. Ellen's tomato rosettes do her proud to this day. And I still marvel at Mother's ability to transform cooking tasks into creative outlets.

Beth, the youngest of us, was often set to making the final flourishes, the little white paper ruffles that were placed on the ends of the turkey drumsticks. Her place cards, done in a childish hand with Pilgrim stick figures, lent bright dots of color to the snow-white tablecloth.

My job was to set the table. I took great care to make sure every knife, spoon, and fork was aligned straight and laid out at exactly the same distance both from the plates and from one another. One year I even checked a book out from the library on fancy ways to fold napkins; startled guests and family were greeted at the table by something that was supposed to look like irises sprouting from the water glasses.

The most awaited person of all was Grandmother. Sailing into the kitchen, she bore before her, like a proud figurehead, a tray with two pies—one mincemeat, the other pumpkin. Grandmother would carefully put her eggbeater and a small metal bowl into the freezer so, as she carefully explained, the well-chilled utensils would create high, firm peaks in her whipped cream.

The many Thanskgivings of my past stretch behind me like a long line of bright candles set on a shining table. There was the one in which we three sisters dressed up as Pilgrims, the one on which my fiancé joined us for the first time. But the Thanksgiving that remains foremost in my mind was the one when I discovered that honest praise could cause miracles to happen.

Painting by Ray App from Ideals Publications

Family and guests had all gathered; grace had been said. The steaming turkey was placed before my father, its basted skin a golden brown. As Dad pierced the glistening russet crust of the turkey, fragrant juices ran down its sides and filled the well at one end of the platter. He carefully sliced thin slivers off the breast and began to stack them on one of Mother's best china plates.

"Don't you think you should save that for last," Grandmother offered, "so that those breast slices will stay warm?"

My father looked up at her. "Probably a good idea, Mother," he replied, and began to spoon out the stuffing into the waiting bowl.

"You probably should hold off a bit on that too, dear," she suggested to her only child. "The warm stuffing will help keep the breast meat hot."

"Hmmm," Dad said noncommittally. He started to carve slices off the sides of the drumsticks.

Conversation began to flow about the table as the cranberry relish was passed, and people complimented my mother on the beautiful turkey.

"Actually, Jim," said Grandmother, "it's a lot easier to carve the legs if you take them both off whole and then slice them onto a side plate."

A small muscle at the side of Dad's mouth began to twitch.

"You know, Dad," I piped up, in what I hoped was a helpful tone, "I think you're carving the turkey just right."

Dad's gaze, which had been fixed in fierce concentration on the turkey, now slowly swept past assembled family and friends and stopped at me. The relish platter paused in mid-pass.

The table grew silent.

"How much is your allowance, Faith?" he asked, pointing at me with the tip of the carving knife.

"Twenty-five cents," I said in a near whisper, sliding down in my seat.

"Excuse me?" he asked, peering at me intently.

"Twenty-five cents a week, Dad," I repeated, forcing my voice through a throat constricted with apprehension.

Looking down the table to my mother, he said, "Joanie, as of today, her allowance is doubled."

"Done," said my mother.

I slumped in my chair with relief and looked at my mother and father. They were grinning at each other. Hesitantly, I raised my eyes to Grandmother's.

She gave me a small smile, then turned to Dad.

"Excellent idea, Jim," she said.

Thanksgiving Day
Each Year Will Be

Loise Pinkerton Fritz

Around the festive tables
The families sit today.
Thankful for each blessing,
They bow their heads and pray
To God who has provided
Each good and perfect gift
Of bounty on each table,
Gifts only He can give.

Around the festal tables
The families sit today.
Grateful for God's goodness,
They give to Him the praise.
Thanksgiving Day each year will be
Because of this one thing:
God's promise of the seedtime
And, too, the harvesting.

Photograph by Larry Lefever/
Grant Heilman Photography, Inc.

THE RURAL LIFE

Verlyn Klinkenborg

To judge by house and yard decorations in the country, Halloween has spilled over its banks and washed away all of October and much of November. In cities, the Christmas season as we know it now—an economic indicator with colored lights and eggnog—can no longer be confined, as it used to be, within the month that begins on the day after Thanksgiving. But Thanksgiving sticks strictly to its allotted Thursday, and the power of this quiet holiday is evident in the trouble so many of us go through to get home in time to honor it. There's something touching about a feast of thanks at which we all find our own reasons to be thankful, in which the feeling is named but not the cause.

The year is getting old and the light weak by the time Thanksgiving comes. The only color in the woods is the green of damp moss and the bright orange berries of bittersweet. There are historic reasons why Thanksgiving falls when it does—matters of Pilgrim fact and presidential proclamation—but, over time, it's become the holiday that defines this bare season. By the end of the eleventh month, the year is ancient enough to have shown us its wisdom. We know what to be grateful for by now, or gratitude is simply beyond us.

You don't have to be very old to remember Thanksgivings that began at four or five in the morning, when women rose alone in the dark to start cooking the turkey. By the time the men and children got out of bed, the bird had already been roasting for a couple of hours on the back porch in its own enameled turkey roaster, a device that lived in the basement all but one day a year, resembled an electric bassinet, and kept the main oven free for pies. Thanksgiving then meant haste in the early hours, a long delay before the big midafternoon dinner, and scratch meals—why eat now?—for breakfast and lunch; a day in which you went straight from starvation to stupefaction, in which men and children felt more than ordinarily useless whenever they came near the kitchen.

Sitting down to the big meal seems like the crux of Thanksgiving, but it really comes a couple of hours later. The pumpkin pie is gone, the dishes are done, the dogs and overnight guests are napping, and there's a strange vacancy in the afternoon light. For a moment the year halts, a moment when the wakeful aren't quite sure what to do with themselves. In that instant, that hollow in time, you find yourself listening to the unnatural stillness of the afternoon, pausing to look closely at the world around you. That's all the celebration necessary on this most modest, most poignant of days.

Aerial view of Peacham, Vermont.
Photograph by William H. Johnson

Bits & Pieces

To make a glorious day complete,
To make each hour full and sweet,
To thank the Lord for life worth living—
That is the real and true Thanksgiving.
—*Abigail Falk*

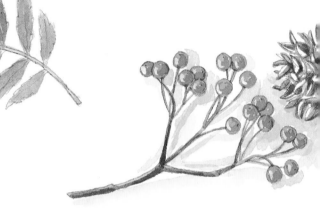

Enter into his gates with thanksgiving, and into his courts with praise: be thankful unto him, and bless his name. For the LORD is good; his mercy is everlasting; and his truth endureth to all generations.
—*Psalm 100:4–5*

But whether we have less or more,
Always thank we God therefor.
—*Author Unknown*

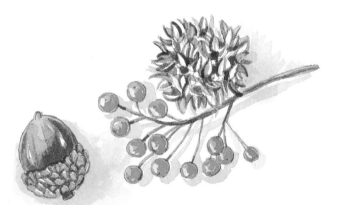

Give thanks unto the LORD, call upon his name, make known his deeds among the people. Sing unto him, sing psalms unto him, talk ye of all his wondrous works.
—*1 Chronicles 16:8–9*

So once in every year we throng
Upon a day apart,
To praise the Lord with feast and song
In thankfulness of heart.
—*Arthur Guiterman*

Remember God's bounty in the year. String the pearls of His favor. Hide the dark parts, except so far as they are breaking out in light! Give this one day to thanks, to joy, to gratitude!
—*Henry Ward Beecher*

Heap high the board with plenteous cheer, and gather to the feast,
And toast the sturdy Pilgrim band whose courage never ceased.
Give praise to that All-Gracious One by whom their steps were led,
And thanks unto the harvest's Lord who sends our daily bread.
—*Alice Williams Brotherton*

For each new morning with its light,
For rest and shelter of the night,
For health and food, for love and friends,
For everything Thy goodness sends.
—*Ralph Waldo Emerson*

NOVEMBER

Gladys Taber

After Thanksgiving dinner, the house simmers down to quiet. It seems cozy and natural to hear muted voices from all over, the baby upstairs waking up, Connie and Don talking, Don's wife tuning the guitar and humming. With all the food around, I reflect comfortably, *We won't need to get another sit-down meal—they can raid.*

Naturally, in a very few hours, there is a kind of stir.

"When are we going to eat?"

"Is it almost supper time?"

"Mind if I eat a little more chestnut stuffing?"

It is very much as it was on Christmas when I said to Jill, "We can have the leftover turkey tomorrow." And she said, "What turkey?"

It turns out there is just enough to slice thin and have cold, plus extra dressing; and, reinforced with a casserole of home-baked beans, nobody perishes of starvation.

"And all of them as thin as pencils," I mourn afterward, "it just isn't fair! They can just eat alarmingly and never gain an ounce. Whereas I—no, no justice at all."

Thanksgiving is far more than the family dinner and national festival. I know all people have always had harvest celebrations of one kind or another, so there is nothing distinctive about a feast-time after the crops are in. But our Thanksgiving seems very close to our relation with God. It has a deep religious significance not always spoken of, but, I think, felt.

I like to slip away for a brief time and sit by the pond on the one bench left out all winter. If it is a warm, hazy day, the sun is slanting over the hill with a gentle glow. If it is cold, the wind walks in the woods. I think of everything I have to be thankful for, and it is a long list by the time it is added up. I am thankful for love and friends and the family gathering together. For starlight over the old apple orchard. For the chilly sweetness of peepers in April. For my winter birds, so brave, so hungry, particularly for my little chickadee with the bent wing that bangs away at the suet cake while I type. He cocks a shining eye at me and seems to say, "Life is really what you make of it, eh?"

I am thankful for music and books. And for the dogs barking at the gate. Well, there are so many things to be thankful for that the list is infinitely long.

And it is good to take time to be thankful.

Country home and barn, East Andover, New Hampshire.
Photograph by William H. Johnson

Featured Poet

Thanksgiving

Eileen Spinelli

Thank you for the world—still sweet.
Thank you for the food we eat.
Thank you for the honeyed-sun
that spoons its light on everyone.
Thank you for the leaves that fall
in glowing piles near the wall,
for kindness in a stranger's face,
and every unexpected grace.
Thank you for the starry dark,
for children laughing in the park,
for cozy towns and sleepy farms,
for dreamers, dancers, babes in arms.
Thank you for all hearts that sing
of hope in spite of everything.

Thanksgiving Song
Stella Craft Tremble

We raise our voice in gratitude for heritage of the past:
For folklore and traditions that our country has amassed,
For the glory of our prairies and the sweep of plain and sea,
For our flag—our nation's emblem of a free democracy!

We thank Thee for the harvests, for November rain and sun,
For peace at frosty winter's edge, for joy in work well-done!
Among the dry sheaves in the fields of tired hearts, we pray,
Plant seeds of joy and gratitude on this Thanksgiving Day!

Be Thankful
Kay Hoffman

The harvest yield is gathered in,
The bins now overflow
With vegetables and fruit and grain
The hand of God bestows.

Here roof and walls are sturdy,
The rooms are snug and warm;
Here faith and love and courage
Help guard against life's storms.

The hill is white for sledding,
Red-cheeked children play;
The smell of turkey fills the air
For it's Thanksgiving Day.

For each dear loved one gathered round
To share the festive board,
For all the blessings that He sends,
Be thankful to our Lord!

Snow-dusted stone wall, Shelburne, Massachusetts.
Photograph by William H. Johnson

Count Our Blessings
Hilda Butler Farr

If we add up our blessings
Upon Thanksgiving Day
We'll find the list is lengthy—
More than we can repay.
Although we've known
    some shadows,
Which come to everyone,
We've also walked in sunshine
And found a share of fun.
So we can learn we're lucky,
Whatever comes our way . . .
If we add up our blessings
Upon Thanksgiving Day.

Gather Your Blessings
Loise Pinkerton Fritz

Gather your blessings
Whatever they are;
Gather, then share them
With those near and far.
Though they be many
Or though they be few,
You'll find that in
sharing them,
God will bless you.

Country store in South Woodstock, Vermont.
Photograph by Dick Dietrich/Dietrich Photography

Thanksgiving

Ella Wheeler Wilcox

We walk on starry fields of white
And do not see the daisies;
For blessings common in our sight,
We rarely offer praises.
We sigh for some supreme delight
To crown our lives with splendor,
And quite ignore our daily store
Of pleasures sweet and tender.

Our cares are bold and push their way
Upon our thought and feeling.
They hang about us all the day,
Our time from pleasure stealing.
So unobtrusive many a joy
We pass by and forget it,
But worry strives to own our lives
And conquers if we let it.

There's not a day in all the year
But holds some hidden pleasure,
And looking back, joys oft appear
To brim the past's wide measure.

But blessings are like friends, I hold,
Who love and labor near us.
We ought to raise our notes of praise
While living hearts can hear us.

Full many a blessing wears the guise
Of worry or of trouble.
Farseeing is the soul, and wise
Who knows the mask is double.
But he who has the faith and strength
To thank his God for sorrow
Has found a joy without alloy
To gladden every morrow.

We ought to make the moments notes
Of happy, glad Thanksgiving;
The hours and days a silent phrase
Of music we are living.
And so the theme should swell and grow
As weeks and months pass o'er us,
And rise sublime at this good time,
A grand Thanksgiving chorus.

Ascension Chapel in Cove, Oregon.
Photograph by Steve Terrill

FIVE GRAINS OF CORN

Claude A. Frazier

The Pilgrims had a custom of putting five grains of corn on each empty plate before a dinner of "thanksgiving" was served. The father, mother, children, and friends would each pick up a grain of corn and tell of something for which they were thankful. The practice reminded them of how the first Pilgrims were in such straits that their allowance was only five grains of corn per person each day. The Pilgrims had little, but they did possess gratitude. It was upon this base of genuine gratitude that America was built.

Gratitude is one of the great virtues. Our English word "thanks" comes from the same Anglo-Saxon word our word "think" does. If we would stop to think, we would pause to be thankful. When we pause to be thankful, we should think of those people we really appreciate—people who have helped us sometime during our life on this earth.

About three years ago, my thoughts turned to the people I especially appreciated. I called each of them. One had been my professor in college; another was a person who had given me a great deal of encouragement; another was one with whom I greatly enjoy playing tennis; and another was a produce-department employee who had been especially helpful to me when I accompanied my wife on our regular Saturday-morning trip to the grocery store. The responses to these calls were amazing and also gratifying. It seems that the calls were the first time someone had expressed appreciation to them in this way. After hearing the enthusiastic responses I was getting from my calls, my wife began to make calls of her own to those persons she particularly appreciated. She encountered the same warm reception I did.

In the case of an especially helpful employee, writing a note to his or her employer or supervisor may be even better than calling. It will be appreciated by the person, and it may even result in a promotion or commendation for the person. For example, my wife and I were in a large department store in New York City. When the closing bell rang, the employees made quick exits—all except one, that is. He had been on his way out, but when he saw us, he laid his overcoat on a chair and helpfully answered questions about the item we were interested in. I asked him if he was a clerk or a manager on that particular floor. "No," was the reply, "I'm a sales clerk on the fifth floor." The next day I made a special trip back to the store manager's office and told him of this incident. I said, "This man treated us as if this were his own personal store." Two weeks later, I got a letter from the store clerk. He thanked me for going to the manager of the store. And he added, "I have been promoted to the position of manager of my floor."

Let us take five grains of corn and think of five people to whom we are especially grateful, and let us tell them how much we appreciate them by a telephone call or a letter on this coming day of Thanksgiving. You may find, as I have found, that the response is so great that you begin thanking people every day.

Photograph by Steve Terrill

THANK YOU, GOD

Bernice Maddux

If my supply of blessings should be shut off this moment, I could not justify complaining about it. I have been the recipient of so many, I could go on giving thanks anyway.

All my life, I have known and basked in the richness of love. All kinds of love. I have been blessed with a loving family and countless close friends who have paved my pathway with gladness and song. I have known young love and old love with a mate I can trust and depend on. I have seen that love reproduce. And witnessed the reproductions of our reproduction.

It's been my pleasure to stroke velvet heads and steal warm kisses from necks of fat babies.

I have raced butterflies through summer, and snowflakes through winter.

I've witnessed thousands of golden sunsets, each one individual, and each more beautiful than the last, it seemed.

And glorious sunrises as they eagerly yanked the covers from the sleeping morning.

I have had my hair pinned back by gentle breezes, and my face caressed by the comforting warmth of the sun.

And showered gently with soft sprays of falling rain.

I have walked barefoot along beaches and let warm, silvery sand sift through my toes.

And across lush carpets of cool, green grass.

It has been my privilege to have drunk from cupped hands from cool springs.

I have walked into the ocean until I dared go no farther and let willing waves slap me all the way back to shore.

I have stood at the top of a mountain and thanked God for it.

I've walked through still woods hand in hand with a small child, letting him stop to show me his world any time he felt like it.

I've stood at rapt attention in the presence of many rainbows and watched until there was nothing left to watch.

I've eaten cold watermelon in the field after a first brisk norther.

And rejoiced as, year after year, dependable hummingbirds gladly return to my doorstep to drink of red nectar.

I hold an all-season ticket to the symphony: a symphony of bird song unlike and far superior to any ever composed by man.

After the fever breaks, I've seen weak smiles and heard the welcome words, "I'm hungry, Mom."

I've always had the comfort and assurance of knowing I was being lovingly watched over by a caring and ever-present God.

I earn my daily bread in a country where I am permitted to think, speak, and act as my heart dictates, as long as I do no harm to others.

All my life I have quenched my thirst at wells I did not dig . . . and I'm most grateful.

If I should never, as long as I live, receive another blessing, I could still say without reservation, "Thank you, God!"

Photograph by Jessie Walker

Let Me Love the Little Things
Loise Pinkerton Fritz

Lord, let me love the little things:
The tiny bird with grayish wings,
The fireflies that shed their light
Amidst the darkness of the night,
The rippling brooks with waters clear
That flow on by from year to year,
The sunset in an evening sky,
The beauty of a butterfly,
The smile upon a small child's face,
A loving family saying grace.
For all the joy these things will bring,
Lord, let me love the little things.

Thanksgiving
Marie Daerr Boehringer

Each has his own Thanksgiving. Some will see
Reason for gladness, noting how the sun
Spills on a last bright branch of barberry,
Or in the joyous way a child will run
Into a mother's arms. There is no rule
For finding bliss. Computers cannot say,
"Here you will find fulfillment," and no school
Can point out happiness. Each finds his way
To peace in his own fashion—sun or sky,
A walk in woods or quiet street, good friends
To talk and laugh with, or the way birds fly,
Trusting, into boughs' shelter when day ends.
Each finds his treasures and his spirit's food—
Then lifts his heart in praise and gratitude.

Photograph by William H. Johnson

Then thank the Lord,

All good gifts around us are sent from heaven above;

O thank the Lord for all His love. Amen. —MATTHIAS CLAUDIAS

Harvest
Gertrude Ryder Bennett

He spoke of harvest, pointed to the field
Where shocks of corn stood boldly in the sun.
The earth was kind to give such lavish yield.
Against the barn were pumpkins piled, each one
A golden promise. Peppers strung and dried
Were red as flame. He took a farmer's pride
In heavy apple trees. He knew the soil.
How well it paid him for a summer's toil!

He spoke of harvest time. She smiled and yet
She hardly heard him. She was gazing where
The children played—a frolicking quartet
Of curls and rompers—and a grateful prayer
Came to her heart. She saw the meaning of
The harvest, felt the strength of boundless love,
Of answered faith. Four children hard at play—
She smiled and brushed a happy tear away.

Thanksgiving
Edgar Daniel Kramer

Dear Lord, for harvests gathered in
And stored away in barn and bin;
For apples, pears; for wool and wheat;
For barley, corn, and honey sweet;
For sun and moon; for snow and rain;
For shifting seasons, hill and plain;
We give Thee thanks!

Photograph by Steve Terrill

This Is Thanksgiving

Richie A. Tankersley

Families close-gathered
with love-gentle faces,
memories of friendships
and warm, special places,
heads bowed in prayer
with hand touching hand,

the smile-to-smile message
each heart understands . . .
This is togetherness,
sharing and living—
This is true happiness . . .
This is Thanksgiving.

ISBN-13: 978-0-8249-1315-1

Published by Ideals Publications, a Guideposts Company
535 Metroplex Drive, Suite 250, Nashville, Tennessee 37211
www.idealsbooks.com

Publisher, Peggy Schaefer
Editor, Melinda Rathjen
Copy Editor, Kaye Dacus
Designer, Marisa Jackson
Permissions Editor, Patsy Jay

Cover: Photograph by Dick Dietrich/Dietrich Photography
Inside front cover: Painting by Donald Mills from Ideals Publications
Inside back cover: Painting by Kenneth Gunall from Ideals Publications

ACKNOWLEDGMENTS:

APPELBAUM, DIANA KARTER. "Menus Through the Years." An excerpt from *Thanksgiving: An American Holiday, An American History.* Copyright © 1984 by Diana Karter Appelbaum. Published by Facts On File Publications. BEDFORD, FAITH ANDREWS. "Carving the Turkey" from *Country Living,* Nov. 2001, Copyright © 2001 Hearst Communications, Inc. BENNETT, GERTRUDE RYDER. "Harvest" from *Homespun,* compiled by Anita Browne, the American Book Company, 1936. Used by permission of the author. BOEHRINGER, MARIE DAERR. "Thanksgiving" from *Sun Press,* November 23. 1978. BORLAND, HAL. "Brown November" from *Sundial of the Seasons* by Hal Borland. Copyright © 1964 by the author, renewed © 1992 by Donal Borland. Used by permission of Frances Collin Literary Agent. FRAZIER, CLAUDE A., M.D. "Five Grains of Corn" from *The Saturday Evening Post.* Copyright © 1989 Saturday Evening Post Society. Used by permission. GALL, ANGELA. "Going Home for Thanksgiving" from *Through Tinted Panes* by Angela Gall. Copyright © 1964 by the author. GOODMAN, ELLEN. "The Keeper of Traditions." An excerpt from *The Family Circle,* Nov. 22, 1994. Copyright © 1994 NYT Women's Magazines. KLINKENBORG, VERLYN. AN EXCERPT from *The Rural Life* by Verlyn Klinkenborg. Copyright © 2002 by the author. Published by Back Bay Books: Little, Brown and Company. MANIER, JOHN. "Thanksgiving" from *Collected Poems, 1966-1997* by John Manier. OAKLEY, HELEN COLWELL. "It's Thanksgiving Day!" An excerpt from *Country Living.* Copyright © 1978 by Helen Oakely. Used by permission of the author. RUTZ, D. SUSAN. "The Color of Thanksgiving." An excerpt from *CAPPER'S,* Nov. 26, 2002, Ogden Publications, Inc. SPINELLI, EILEEN. "Thanksgiving." Previously published in *GRIT.* Used by permission of the author. TABER, GLADYS. "November" from *Stillmeadow Calendar.* Copyright © 1967 by Gladys Taber, renewed 1995 by Constance Colby Taber. Used by permission of Brandt and Hochman Literary Agents, Inc. THOMPSON, KAREN PILIBOSIAN. "The Truth About Turkey Soup" from *Country Living,* November 1998. Our sincere thanks to the following authors or their heirs, some of whom we may have been unable to locate: June Masters Bacher, Esther York Burkholder , Hilda Butler Farr, Inez Franck, Loise Pinkerton Fritz, Mona K. Guldswog, Kay Hoffman, Pamela Kennedy, Edgar Daniel Kramer, Bernice Maddux, Virginia Blanck Moore, Wilbur Dick Nesbit, Ruth Pitcher, Margaret L. Rorke, Richie A. Tankersley, and Stella Craft Tremble. Every effort has been made to establish ownership and use of each selection in this book. If contacted, the publisher will be pleased to rectify any inadvertent errors or omissions in subsequent reprints.